with God

for Grandparents

PRAYERS FOR EVERY GRANDPARENT

KEL GROSECLOSE

DIMENSIONS
FOR LIVING
NASHVILLE

A Moment with God for Grandparents:
Prayers for Every Grandparent

Copyright © 1999 by Dimensions for Living

This book is printed on acid-free paper.

Library of Congress Cataloging-in-Publication Data

Groseclose, Kel, 1940–
    A moment with God for grandparents: prayers for every grandparent/Kel Groseclose.
        p.   cm.
    ISBN 0-687-97560-3 (alk. paper)
    1. Grandparents—Prayer-books and devotions—English.   I. Title.
BV4845.G73   1999
242'.845—dc21
                                                            98-50447
                                                                CIP

99 00 01 02 03 04 05 06 07 08 — 10 9 8 7 6 5 4 3 2 1

MANUFACTURED IN THE UNITED STATES OF AMERICA

CONTENTS

EXPECTANT GRANDPARENTS

Creation waits with eager longing for the revealing of the children of God.
                              —Romans 8:19

Gracious God, Grandma and I are two members of creation who wait with eager longing for the revealing of more grandchildren. We already have five, but we'd like many more. We're not being greedy. It's just that they bring us such joy!

You were wise not to let grandparents be part of that decision. All we can do is wait patiently, pray faithfully, and offer gentle words of encouragement to our children and their spouses. Perhaps you could speed up the process if you'd whisper in their ears and speak to their hearts. We'd really like to be expectant grandparents again.

THOSE BLESSED BEGATS

Abraham begat Isaac; and Isaac begat Jacob; and Jacob begat Judas and his brethren. —*Matthew 1:2 KJV*

Creator God, look what you started in that garden with Adam and Eve! They started the "begatting" process, and several millennia later we're still going strong. As long as your people are responsible in how this happens and caring in the way they raise the results, I think it's a wonderful plan.

Our immediate family was gifted with six offspring. Five of those are married and have produced five grandchildren. It's good to know this was your idea in the first place and that we're part of an endless line of blessed begats. Thank you, God; it gives us comfort and courage.

GIFTS FROM GOD

❧

Little children, you are from God.
—*1 John 4:4*a

Yes, indeed, children in general and grandchildren in particular are gifts from you, O God; and very special gifts, at that. I happen to think that *this* Grandma and Grandpa's grandkids are the cutest, brightest, sweetest, and most-talented youngsters in the world. That's what I'm supposed to believe. You don't expect me to be objective, do you? I'm their number one fan, their loudest cheerleader, and their most loyal supporter—next to you, of course, Lord. What's wonderful is you've also made it so that *every* grandparent can have the best grandchildren in all the world. What a clever and diplomatic God you are!

WE GATHER TOGETHER

Blow the trumpet in Zion; sanctify a fast; / call a solemn assembly; / gather the people. / [A]ssemble the aged; / gather the children, / even infants at the breast. —Joel 2:15-16

Eternal Parent, this text sounds like one of our family gatherings, except we're seldom solemn and don't ever fast; there's usually a ton of food. Whether we eat or not, our family gatherings are significant events. Everybody talks at once yet somehow hears everything. We catch up on the latest news, see how much the grandchildren have grown, and stay up too late. We give and receive multitudes of hugs and kisses. When it's over, our house is a mess and our bodies are weary. But our grandparent souls are crammed with happiness, overflowing with joy. O God, provide us with another reason to gather, and make it soon.

THE ALPHA AND THE OMEGA

Then he said to me, "It is done! I am the Alpha and the Omega, the beginning and the end."

—Revelation 21:6a, b

There's a unique bond, O God, between the youngest and the oldest members of the human race. Sometimes it almost seems as if we're in cahoots with one another. We have this common understanding about what really matters in life. It's not about making money, driving a new car, keeping your bedroom clean, or eating your vegetables. It's about being together, loving one another, and finding joy every day. So this grandpa blows soap bubbles with grandchildren until his elbows are soaking wet, gives wheelbarrow rides until his back is stiff, and watches butterflies gracefully sip from flowers; call it my second childhood, if you like. I call it marvelous!

THE "GOOD OLD DAYS" MYTH

Don't long for "the good old days," for you don't know whether they were any better than these!

—Ecclesiastes 7:10 TLB

O God, it's tempting for us grandparents to glorify the past, to believe it actually was as wonderful as those stories we tell about it. Yes, we've had wonderful times in bygone days, but there were plenty of struggles too. Help us increasingly mature individuals to both cherish our memories and to accept the changes and challenges of the present moment. May we regale our grandchildren with tales of our personal histories, yet be alive with them here and now.

This is the day you've made for us, Lord, not yesterday (Psalm 118:24). Let us rejoice and make *these* the "good NEW days"!

CHOOSING
YOUR OWN WRINKLES

The lines are fallen unto me in pleasant places; yea, I have a goodly heritage.
—*Psalm 16:6 KJV*

O God of the Ages and the aging, I know this Scripture refers to property boundary lines. But suppose it also has a message for faces like mine that show the effects of having lived quite a while. Though I may not have a choice about getting wrinkles, I can decide to put them in pleasant places. I have a few worry wrinkles etched across my forehead. But, Lord, you and I have placed other facial lines in good spots—those happy crinkles around the corners of my eyes, the smile creases beside my mouth. Now when a grandchild innocently asks, "Grandpa, where'd you get all your wrinkles?" I shall reply, "From God. Aren't they beautiful?"

GRANDCHILDREN SPOILED WHILE YOU WAIT

❧

"Give, and it will be given to you. A good measure, pressed down, shaken together, running over, will be put into your lap."
—Luke 6:38a, b

O God, you have given us every good and perfect gift, lavished your love upon us, and basically spoiled us with an abundance of beauty, with promises and hope and joy. So why shouldn't we grandparents be able to spoil our grandkids? I don't mean we should spoil them rotten by providing every material thing their hearts desire or by letting them get away with unpleasant behavior. You don't cater to our selfish whims or condone our unloving attitudes; nor should we with our grandchildren. But we *can* shower spiritual blessings upon them and be extravagant in offering our love.

AN INSIDE JOB

God can do anything, you know—far more than you could ever imagine or guess or request in your wildest dreams! He does it not by pushing us around but by working within us, his Spirit deeply and gently within us.
—Ephesians 3:20 The Message

Remind me, Gracious God, that grandchildren are gifts to be cherished. You haven't given them to me to make me look good or feel important. They're not on this earth so my billfold can be filled with a zillion pictures. Nor is their purpose to make me proud of their grades, athletic prowess, musical talents, or any other outward accomplishment; that's all gravy. Help this grandparent never to push from the outside and always to nurture from the inside. May I be your Spirit's partner in gently bringing out the best in my grandchildren.

WHEN YOU CAN'T GET YOUR HANDS ON THEM

So the LORD *scattered them abroad from there over the face of all the earth.*
—*Genesis 11:8a*

Maybe it's not you who is doing the scattering anymore, Lord, but people today certainly don't stay close to home. We've got family members across the mountains in Seattle, one in New Jersey, and another one up North; it is difficult for us to "get our hands on" our grandchildren—to be able to spend time with them. And too, they're busy with their work and activities. I know we can always hold them in our hearts, and we do. But sometimes our laps feel empty and our arms get lonely. In the meantime, we send cards, e-mail, talk on the telephone, share photographs, and remember them constantly in our prayers. And we yearn for that time when we can be physically with them again.

THE STRENGTH
OF SITTING STILL

❦

Their strength is to sit still.
—Isaiah 30:7b KJV

The prophet Isaiah thought it was a weakness of the Egyptians, and perhaps in battle it is. But, Dear God, for grandparents, sitting can be a source of strength. We may not have as much energy as we once had. Our "get-up-and-go" may have gotten up and gone. We have other gifts to offer, though, such as stability, confidence, and quietness.

The day is surely coming when I shall have to trade my "Super Gramps" T-shirt for something more modest; so be it. Let me sit in a rocking chair and snuggle with my grandchildren and perhaps my great-grandchildren. I'll listen, watch them play, read books while they sit on my lap, and be very content.

THE CARE AND FEEDING OF GRANDPARENTS

You shall be happy, and it shall go well with you. / . . . May you see your children's children.

—*Psalm 128:2b, 6a*

This is a kindly reminder, isn't it God, for us to take proper care of our bodies. We want to live long enough to see our children's children—that is, to become grandparents—and to have adequate strength and health to enjoy the experience. Make no mistake about it, those grandchildren need us to be there for them too.

Motivate me, Lord, to eat nutritiously, to exercise regularly, to get enough sleep, and to go to the doctor for checkups. There are others, perhaps quite a number, who value my wisdom, enjoy my company, and need my love. So help this "old man" to take care of himself!

LONGITUDINAL WISDOM

I have been young, and now am old, / yet I have not seen the righteous forsaken / or their children begging bread.

—Psalm 37:25

O God, you probably thought up the idea of grandparents to keep society optimistic. We do bring a certain healthy perspective based on years of experience. We've seen a lot, had some tough times, and are convinced of your faithfulness. No matter what happens, we've been around long enough to know we're never alone; you are our constant companion. We're able to see the big picture, the historical view. We don't get upset over short-term troubles, because *you* are in this for the long haul. Anyway, from your point of view, a thousand years are but as yesterday (Psalm 90:4). Teach us to relax, to cherish each moment, and to trust you completely.

HOW MUCH YOU'VE GROWN

Grow in the grace and knowledge of our Lord and Savior Jesus Christ.

—*2 Peter 3:18*

As a child I used to dread our large extended-family gatherings. I enjoyed the food, running around with cousins, and my Aunt Hettie's homemade chocolates. I barely tolerated, however, those repeated pats on my head while a grandparent exclaimed, "My, how much you've grown! Just like a weed. You'll soon be taller than your daddy."

Well, now, God of grace and glory, somebody ought to be checking on us grandparents to see how much we've grown; not in girth, of course, but in faith and love. Those pats on top of my head I can still do without. But, Dear God, keep close track of my growth in faith and in the knowledge of your Son Jesus Christ.

BLESSED ARE THE PLAYFUL

Thus says the LORD of hosts: Old men and old women shall again sit in the streets of Jerusalem. . . . And the streets of the city shall be full of boys and girls playing.
—*Zechariah 8:4-5*

O God, I had quite a mother, didn't I? She was the neighborhood granny. Kids came from blocks away to visit her. She entertained them royally. I suppose she was lonely living there alone after my father's death, though she handled it well. Her place was always filled with children playing "button, button, who's got the button," hide-the-thimble, and other old-fashioned games. Mother read to the children, visited with them, and always served a delicious snack before they left. She was playful to the very end. May our homes and streets be filled again with older folks and children at play.

THE ART OF NAPPING

So the L<small>ORD</small> *God caused a deep sleep to fall upon the man, and he slept.*
—*Genesis 2:21a*

Things haven't changed much since Adam, have they Lord? You, of course, caused the first man to nod off; so maybe it's *still* because of you that we males, especially us grandpas, have perfected the art of napping. I prefer to think we're not lazy; we're simply setting a good example for our youngest grandchildren who need their naps! We grandpas are witnessing to the value and joy of dozing in a comfortable chair. We know that some things cannot be hurried and that patience is a virtue. Not to mention that our snoring provides a wonderful source for family laughter! The closest experience to heaven may be napping on the couch while holding a sleeping grandchild.

A LEGACY OF FAITH

I am reminded of your sincere faith, a faith that lived first in your grandmother Lois and your mother Eunice and now, I am sure, lives in you.

—2 Timothy 1:5

Wouldn't I like to leave my grandchildren the kind of legacy Lois left for Timothy! She passed on to her daughter and grandson a genuine and sincere faith. I'd be pleased to share a bit of material wealth with my family, to hand to them my treasured possessions. When it comes to inner, spiritual values, however, there's no comparison.

May I not be concerned about my bank account and stock portfolio so much as what's in my heart. May I leave my grandchildren a legacy of hope and peace, of caring and compassion. Let me be formed in the Lois mold of grandparenting. And may I accomplish all this with a minimum of sermonettes.

OLD DOGS CAN LEARN
NEW TRICKS

And the one who was seated on the throne said, "See, I am making all things new."
　　　　　　　　　　—Revelation 21:5a

Lord, if in the next life we shall all be made new, shouldn't we be preparing for it in this one? Even we old dogs, we grandparents, ought to be learning a few new tricks. It's possible; it just takes us a little longer.

O God of time and eternity, keep this grandfather's eyes open, his ears attentive, his mind receptive, and his body willing. May I never stop learning. Thank you for providing me with the best of all teachers—my grandchildren. They lovingly insist that I practice my new tricks; they won't let this old dog sit and vegetate!

GREAT-GRANNY'S STAR

He determines the number of the stars; / he gives to all of them their names.
—*Psalm 147:4*

It was a difficult experience for us all. But you, O God, comforted us with the wisdom of a three-year-old granddaughter. You knew how much it hurt when Great-Granny died, so you sent Ashley to be with us. We gathered at our house. Ashley's family brought McDonald's burgers; and while we ate, we hugged, cried, and felt lonely together. When Ashley went home that evening, she looked into the night sky, found the first star, and blew it a kiss. "Why are you doing that?" her mother asked. "Because," she replied confidently, "Great-Granny's in heaven, and that's her star." I hope it's also permissible for a grandpa to blow kisses to a star.

STANDING IN THE GAP

And I sought for [one] among them, that should . . . stand in the gap before me for the land.
—Ezekiel 22:30a KJV, adapted

Grandparents are great for standing in the gap. No, not the clothing store that's popular with young people, although I've done my share of waiting there. I mean the role of being ready to step in when their parents need help. Our grandchildren all have a mom and dad who work outside the home.

If you aren't going to slow down the pace of this world, O God, then please, start calling more grandparents into the "gap standing" business. We're not cheap labor; we're active family elders who care. When emergencies occur, troubles happen, or parents are at their wit's end, make us willing to stand humbly in the gap.

DOING WHAT IS POSSIBLE

*If you wait for perfect conditions, you will
never get anything done.*
—*Ecclesiastes 11:4 TLB*

Forgive me, O God of infinite patience,
for too often waiting for perfection before
I act. I postpone doing anything until I'm
certain there's enough money, time, and
energy. I want gorgeous weather, detailed
plans, and agreeable grandchildren. It's not
going to happen, is it, Lord? Neither you
nor they are impressed that I'm now the
family patriarch and in charge around here.

Please send me a clear message, Lord;
blow a loud horn in my ear, if you have to.
Help me become more flexible,
spontaneous, and adventurous. The image
of a cautious, cranky grandfather isn't
flattering. I may never be a wild and crazy
guy, but I'd like my grandchildren to
think I'm a good sport.

THE OLD STORYTELLER

*My child, be attentive to my words; / incline
your ear to my sayings.*

—*Proverbs 4:20*

O God, I don't know if you laugh at
jokes I've repeatedly told, but my
grandchildren do. They may roll their eyes
and wink at their parents, yet they still
chuckle. Maybe they're giggling at my
forgetfulness more than at the punchline.
Whatever, I appreciate their attentiveness
and good manners. After all, Lord, I did
the same for my grandparents. I fidgeted,
but I listened respectfully as my grandpa
spun tales of when there were no cars and
he rode a horse; of a one-room
schoolhouse; or of seeing his first airplane.

Books aren't the only source of history.
We grandparents have a wealth of
information and wisdom. Help us not to
bore our grandchildren by repeating our
stories too often.

GRANDCHILDREN GIVE PRECIOUS GIFTS

"Whoever becomes humble like this child is the greatest in the kingdom of heaven."
—*Matthew 18:4*

O God, keep me humble, lest I think I'm the giver and my grandchildren are the receivers. If truth be told, they give me the most wonderful gift of all. As I welcome them, they offer me nothing less than your son, Jesus. I may give them piggyback rides, ice-cream cones, and birthday gifts. They give me life: dandelion bouquets, sticky lollipops, artwork for the refrigerator, spiritual openness, renewed energy, laughter and joy, hope for the future.

O Lord, my grandchildren hold in their hearts the secret to gaining entrance into eternity. May I always receive their gifts with thankfulness.

LOVE BEARS AND BELIEVES

[Love] bears all things, believes all things. . . .
—1 Corinthians 13:7a

Dear God, our grandson Tyler is a sweet boy. He's six now, and very handsome. I love those freckles sprinkled across his cute nose and how his eyes crinkle in the corners from smiling so much. But, as you know, there's one thing that brings pain to his grandparents' hearts: He's autistic, and all his words and memories are trapped inside his brain. His loving parents have graciously accepted his condition and are wonderful with him. We know how very much you love Tyler, and we believe you have special things in store for him. As he grows, please help us love him with patience and kindness; and may your Spirit give us deep within the conviction that love "bears all things, believes all things."

LOVE HOPES AND ENDURES

. . . [Love] hopes all things, endures all things. —*1 Corinthians 13:7b*

Lord, you know I seldom ask for favors. I try to seek your will, to trust your guidance and praise your name. But there are so many illnesses in this wide world, so many grandchildren who are hurting or are in the dark in some way. Please raise the awareness and stir the hearts of people everywhere to give of their time and money so that more research can be done and solutions found for impairing conditions such as autism. I don't mean to be selfish, but I'd like it to come soon enough to help Tyler.

He receives wonderful care, both from his parents and his doctors. Don't think we aren't grateful; we are! But our love can't seem to quit hoping for a breakthrough. We thank you, Lord, for understanding how we feel.

THE GREATEST GIFT OF ALL

❧

Faith, hope, and love abide, these three; and the greatest of these is love.
—*1 Corinthians 13:13*

Love is your eternal gift. *These* particular grandparents believe with every fiber of their being that love is absolutely the greatest! We experience it in overflowing measure from all of our grandchildren. I thank you now, O God, for the unique quality of love as we receive it from Tyler. As he holds our hands and gives us hugs and squeezes, it sometimes seems as though they have come directly from you. With no words to express his love, he finds other ways: mushy kisses, giggles, tickles, and face rubs. We are grateful for Jesus' love, which is so transparent in our Tyler!

GREATER THAN THE SUM OF ITS PARTS

Two are better than one, because they have a good reward for their toil. For if they fall, one will lift up the other.
—*Ecclesiastes 4:9-10*a

Thank you, God, for creating the extended family. In the stress of today's hectic pace, we need to work together. It's sort of like changing bed sheets: Two people can do the job more than twice as easily as one. One person alone would get weary running from side to side.

It's the same in raising children. We need to encourage one another. We're a team. If somebody stumbles or falls, another can lift them up. And we grandparents are a vital part of that team. We bring years of experience, emotional support, prayer power, and, when possible, a wonderful ministry of presence.

A CLAY JAR GRANDPA

But we have this treasure in clay jars, so that it may be made clear that this extraordinary power belongs to God and does not come from us.
—*2 Corinthians 4:7*

O God, you're looking at a most imperfect grandparent—me. By myself, I cannot be the grandfather I yearn to be. This is the man, remember, with a round tummy, thinning hair, and tired muscles from chasing two granddaughters around the backyard for hours. There are days when I feel like an ancient clay pot. Inside of me, however, you've placed a treasure! You've filled me with patience, spiritual endurance, inner peace and joy. I've got your divine love filling up this old body. What a wise God you are!

TOO DEEP FOR WORDS

The Spirit helps us in our weakness; for we do not know how to pray as we ought, but that very Spirit intercedes with sighs too deep for words. —Romans 8:26

Your Spirit has given to grandparents the gift of sighing. Young persons don't do it well; it takes years of practice. Actually, sighing is a form of prayer. There are deep problems and profound joys that words simply cannot capture. We grandparents understand that, and this Scripture tells us that you do too.

Sighs cannot be programmed. They are spontaneous expressions of weariness or ecstasy, of resignation or acceptance, of emptiness or fullness. They are best done while sitting in a comfortable rocking chair or in a warm bath, and they should involve one's whole body and soul. Show me a loving grandparent, O God, and I'll show you an accomplished "sigher."

THE NUMBERS GAME

Though [one] lives a thousand years twice over, but doesn't find contentment—well, what's the use?
　　　　—Ecclesiastes 6:6 TLB, adapted

Are you saying, O God, that how long we live isn't as important as what we do with the time we have; that it's quality, not quantity, that counts? Should we be striving for inner contentment, not just for outward accomplishment? You don't care, do you, whether we have one grandchild or dozens. Bragging rights are good for nothing. What matters is our loving relationship with each grandchild. It's not about how much money we spend on them; it's how much of ourselves we give.

Thank you, Lord, for this helpful reminder. I may need it again soon.

A GREAT CLOUD
OF GRANDPARENTS

❦

Therefore, since we are surrounded by so great a cloud of witnesses, . . . let us run with perseverance the race that is set before us, looking to Jesus.
—*Hebrews 12:1-2a*

When Great-Granny died in late August, little Lexie was not yet a year old. They'd been together on occasion, but Great-Granny was very ill, and quality time together was limited. One day that next summer, when Lexie and her mother (our daughter) were visiting with Grandma and their Aunt Sara in our family room, a gust of wind blew through the open family room door. Twenty-one-month-old Lexie, looking toward the breeze, said loudly and plainly, "Hi, Great-Granny!" Yes, granddaughter, there is indeed a great cloud of witnesses, including a host of heavenly grandparents. Enjoy them!

IT'S ALWAYS THE SEASON
FOR LOVING

*For everything there is a season, and a time
for every matter under heaven.*
—*Ecclesiastes 3:1*

O God, there were all those years of parenting, and they were good years, but now it's the season of grandparenting. There's a time for offering advice, and a time for keeping silent; a time to do things for them, and a time to let them do for themselves; a time to send money, and a time not to send money; a time to be with them, and a time to give them space. But, Dear God, it's always the season for *loving* them.

WRITTEN IN THEIR HEARTS

I will put my law within them, and I will write it on their hearts; and I will be their God, and they shall be my people.
—Jeremiah 31:33b, c

Thank you, O God of our soul's deep places, for giving grandparents the ability to speak heart language. It's not our gift alone; but if we're retired and freed from working outside the home, we have the possibility of focusing on the inner life. We may have more time than when we were actively parenting to be quiet and meditative, to appreciate the beauty of creation. Hopefully, we're also more mature and at peace with ourselves. Encourage us to use the language of love with our grandchildren so that your Word might become written on their hearts.

BLESSED OFFSPRING

They shall not labor in vain, / or bear children for calamity; / for they shall be offspring blessed by the LORD— / and their descendants as well.

—*Isaiah 65:23*

Help us, Dear God, to create a society where our children and grandchildren can live in security and safety, where opportunities abound and joy is an everyday occurrence. Remind us older generations that we have a vital role to play in this process. We must speak out for justice and equality, witness for peace, pray for reconciliation of peoples, and seek a revival of the Spirit in our world. If we do so, it will matter little whether we're still around to enjoy the fruits of our labor. We will have a group of wonderful individuals following in our footsteps—our beloved grandchildren!

A PLACE APART

Jesus took with him Peter and James and John, and led them up a high mountain apart, by themselves.

—Mark 9:2a

Leaving our usual routine and going to a special place can be an effective way of growing closer together. Your Son and three of his disciples went mountain climbing. My parents used to take our children fishing and backpacking. We play with our grandchildren in the park, go for walks in the rain, have picnic lunches, blow soap bubbles, and volunteer at their Bible school. The possibilities are limited only by our imagination. There's the library, the zoo, movies, toy stores, backyard tenting, treehouses, tea parties, bicycle rides, and who knows what else. Lord, staying together by going apart is a good job for grandparents.

BOUND IN THE BUNDLE

❧

*[We] shall be bound in the bundle of the
living under the care of the* Lord *[our]
God.*

—*1 Samuel 25:29*b, *adapted*

I may be a one-of-a-kind grandfather,
but I'm still "bound in the bundle of the
living." I'm part of a whole world of
grandparents from every culture and land,
with different languages and customs.
We're basically all the same: We love our
grandchildren with all our heart and want
the very best for them. We burst with
pride at their accomplishments, worry
over their struggles, and pray for your
blessings upon them. Thank you, God,
for binding us grandparents in this great
bundle of humanity and for connecting all
of us by your love.

NO FAVORITISM HERE

The wisdom from above is first pure, then peaceable, gentle, willing to yield, full of mercy and good fruits, without a trace of partiality or hypocrisy.

—James 3:17

Amen, Lord! I totally agree. So does my spouse, a.k.a. "Grandma." You've given her a strong sense of fairness and equal treatment. It's a quality she's passed on to several of our children. If I brag about one grandchild, I'm quickly reminded to say kind words about the other four. If I write about one, I had better write about them all. We spend about the same amount of money on them for birthdays and at Christmas. They're each unique individuals (my, are they ever!), and we honor that. To the best of our human ability, they're equally valued and equally loved.

REMEMBER THE DAYS OF OLD

Remember the days of old, / consider the years long past; / ask your father, and he will inform you; / your elders, and they will tell you.
—*Deuteronomy 32:7*

A sense of history is important for everybody; and much of it can't be learned from textbooks, especially the history of one's own family. I learned this from climbing into the attic of my grandparents' house in rural Idaho. There were old trunks filled with Civil War memorabilia: uniforms and medals, letters and tintypes. Their house was a fascinating place. I remember the wood stove in the kitchen, and Grandpa in his garden, weeding the cantaloupe patch. These memories and many others help me feel connected to the past and give me confidence in the future. O God, help me provide our grandchildren with rich family memories of their own.

FULL OF SAP

In old age they still produce fruit; / they are always green and full of sap.
—Psalm 92:14

That's me, O Lord: full of sap. I'm still going strong, producing fruit, and staying green. I guess I'm like one of those palm trees or cedars of Lebanon.

Old age isn't so bad, especially if being a grandparent is part of the deal. I can't run as fast or jump as high, but I'm producing a bountiful harvest. I'm more seasoned, more patient, and a lot wiser. It's good to be full of sap—to be enthusiastic about life, to be growing in faith, increasing in love. It takes me longer to get out of bed each morning, but once I get my sap going I can almost keep pace with my grandchildren.

NO SUCH PLACE AS FAR AWAY

Now you belong to Christ Jesus, and though you once were far away from God, now you have been brought very near to him.
—*Ephesians 2:13 TLB*

O God, we are close to you because of One who loved and gave himself for us. Help us to be close to our grandchildren who live far away, to love and give ourselves to them. Corey and Haley are super grandkids, full of energy and with lots of ideas for keeping their grandparents busy. But they live across a range of high mountains, and with everybody's busy schedules, we don't see them often enough. Whether they are far or near geographically, they're always in our memories and close to our hearts. In the Spirit realm, there's no such place as far away.

HOLD FAST
TO THE TRADITIONS

*Stand firm and hold fast to the traditions
that you were taught by us.*
—*2 Thessalonians 2:15*

You are the God both of change and constancy, of new creations and traditions; apparently, you don't see any conflict of interest there. Maybe it's possible for us to hold fast to our family traditions without becoming squinty-eyed, pinched-mouth grandparents. Lord, you know how many traditions we have in this clan, from using the same Christmas tree ornaments and tattered Easter baskets year after year to hand-cranking ice cream on the Fourth of July; the list is long. But these things give us a sense of continuity, provide a platform for the future, and bring us many tears and much laughter.

TIMES OF REFRESHING

"Repent therefore, and turn to God so that your sins may be wiped out, so that times of refreshing may come from the presence of the Lord."

—*Acts 3:19-20a*

It had been a long winter, Lord. During the night, it quietly, secretly snowed. I'd already done my quota of shoveling and wasn't amused. Ashley, barely two at the time, arrived for a visit just as I was starting to scrape the sidewalk. "Oh, please, Grandma, may I help Grandpa?" Hat and gloves were found, and out she came, eyes sparkling. She scooped handfuls of snow and threw it into the air while joyously exclaiming, "Yes! Yes! Oh, yes!" She paused, looked skyward, and said with reverence, "It's a new day!" I quit complaining on the spot.

OLD-FASHIONED VALUES FOR NEWFANGLED GRANDKIDS

❧

Jesus Christ is the same yesterday and today and forever. —Hebrews 13:8

O God, the world today is changing faster than some of us grandparents can keep pace. Learning computer language and programming a VCR can be major challenges for people of our generation. Rapid change is part of contemporary life. We should at least try to keep up-to-date.

This doesn't mean, however, that the Ten Commandments ought to be discarded or that the Golden Rule is passé. Jesus Christ and his teachings are as applicable as ever. So are the values he espoused—faithfulness, honesty, truthfulness, stewardship, caring, love. These have been around a long while, yet they're always in season. God, are you depending on grandparents to teach these qualities?

PRAY ABOUT EVERYTHING

Don't worry about anything; instead, pray about everything.
—*Philippians 4:6*a, b *TLB*

O God, you already know how often I chew on the skin beside my fingernails. My mother tried to make me stop, but to no avail. When I get nervous, it just seems to help. I don't, however, do it in public. I should simply trust you, Creator of the universe, to take complete care of things. Instead of worrying about anything, you invite me to pray about everything.

With grandchildren, I have more concerns and anxieties. All the more reason to pray. Remind me of prayer's power and how it blesses my family. My fingers would probably appreciate it too.

THE GIFT OF SELF

They voluntarily gave according to their means . . . ; they gave themselves first to the Lord and, by the will of God, to us.
                    —2 Corinthians 8:3, 5

First, we must give ourselves to you, O God, and then to each other before we're ready to offer outward gifts. The best present grandparents can give is their personality, their soul. Cash or candy, a balloon or bicycle—these are soon gone. A lifetime relationship comes through the giving of one's heart.

We don't need to impress, but rather to *bless* our grandchildren. There are no substitutes for genuine caring, faithfulness, commitment, and unconditional love. Grandchildren usually accept our visible tokens and trinkets. But what they truly need is for us to give to them *ourselves*.

PERMISSION TO BE CHARACTERS

We also boast in our sufferings, knowing that suffering produces endurance, and endurance produces character, and character produces hope, and hope does not disappoint us.
—Romans 5:3-5

Thank you, God, for permitting us, even encouraging us, to be unique individuals. My own grandparents both *had* character and *were* characters. They had their little habits that irritated or embarrassed me. One grandmother's false teeth clicked loudly when she ate; my maternal grandfather always removed his shoes in the evening and picked his toes, no matter who was visiting. I imagine my grandchildren have noticed a few faults in me. Yet they accept me for the character I am. I do the same for them; it's called *family*.

KNOCKED DOWN
BUT NOT OUT

We may be knocked down but we are never knocked out!
—2 Corinthians 4:9 JBP

Kind and nurturing Spirit, you know how often I've taken a tumble. My life's been very good, yet I've been knocked down occasionally. I've had my share of failures, disappointments, and grief. I've gotten my lumps, but I've never been knocked out. In each case you've picked me up, dusted me off, and sent me on my way. You've restored my soul!

As you know, grandparents don't bounce off the floor as quickly as their grandchildren do. Next time I get flattened, O God, please be patient. It takes my muscles and bones a little longer these days to get up and get going again.

LIFE IS SWEET

My child, eat honey, for it is good, / and the drippings of the honeycomb are sweet to your taste. / Know that wisdom is such to your soul.
—*Proverbs 24:13-14a*

My Aunt Hettie lived next door to my grandparents in Oregon. She was a severe-looking woman, and cranky too. My dilemma was that she made the most delicious candy I'd ever tasted—Rocky Road, divinity, fudge, and peanut brittle. I was scared of her, but my sweet tooth always prevailed. I spent considerable time at her house.

Rabbis of old used a similar ploy: After students learned a passage from the Torah, a drop of honey was placed on their tongues. O God, even when things are tough, I want our grandchildren to know how sweet and precious life is.

IN PRAISE OF SIMPLICITY

He that giveth, let him do it with simplicity.
—Romans 12:8b KJV

The happiest moments and most cherished gifts are often the simplest. Maybe that's why you, O God, sent your love to us as a baby born in a manger. You couldn't have done it more humbly if you'd tried. It reminds me of how a child will set aside the gift and play with the cardboard box instead.

You deal with us in such basic ways—a gentle touch, a sweet lullaby, a quiet prayer, a walk in the garden. Help me as a grandparent to offer myself with purity, sincerity, and humility. Let me give my love freely and with simplicity.

A PRAYER FOR
FULL-TIME GRANDPARENTS

Take a new grip with your tired hands, stand firm on your shaky legs, and mark out a straight, smooth path for your feet.
—*Hebrews 12:12-13a TLB*

Dear God, quite a number of grandparents have by necessity been pressed into duty as surrogate parents for their grandchildren. Give them an extra measure of your strength. It's wonderful that they can do so, but it's not an easy job. Child-rearing was quite a responsibility even when they were younger. Compensate, O God, for their lack of physical energy with the wisdom of experience and the confidence of maturity; and let them know they're surrounded by the love and prayers of all the other grandparents in this world.

IMPROVING WITH AGE

So we do not lose heart. Even though our outer nature is wasting away, our inner nature is being renewed day by day.
—2 Corinthians 4:16

My outer nature is indeed wasting away, slowly but surely eroding. My eyes aren't as good, and my hearing is not as sharp. I've still got my own teeth, but they're held together by bridgework. I've got hair, just not as much as you originally gave me. Nevertheless, there's great joy in growing older, for you are renewing our inner nature day by day. That blesses us here and now, and also eternally.

Clearly, O God, you use grandchildren as part of your daily renewal process. They bring us such joy that our grandparently souls can't help but be restored. Amen!

SECURITY AND SUPPORT

He gives them security, and they are supported; / his eyes are upon their ways.
—*Job 24:23*

O Advocate and Comforter of your people, help us to provide a secure environment for all children, including our grandchildren. Every child on this earth deserves support and encouragement. These aren't easy times in which to grow up. The pressures are intense, the problems large, and the dangers great. May we provide a place where our grandchildren feel safe and secure. May our eyes be "upon" them. May we watch over them yet not smother them. Grant them awareness of the risks, yet let them not live in fear. Dear God, give parents and grandparents wisdom to direct and protect their beloved offspring without limiting their freedom to explore.

IN PRAISE OF
DEPENDABILITY

❧

"I will never completely take away my lovingkindness from them, nor let my promise fail. No, I will not break my covenant; I will not take back one word of what I said."
—Psalm 89:33-34 TLB

Your covenant of love, O God, is set in concrete. It's so permanent, there's absolutely nothing that can separate us from it. What a wonderful feeling! We humans struggle to be faithful and dependable. We break promises we've made to you and to one another. We say we'll do something, then we neglect to follow through. Motivate me as a grandparent to be consistent and constant, trustworthy and true, faithful and firm.

HARVEST OF THE SOUL

The fruit of the Spirit is love, joy, peace, patience, kindness, generosity, faithfulness, gentleness, and self-control.
—Galatians 5:22-23a

Finally, Dear God, finally it is harvest season for my soul. As a grandparent I'm actually bearing fruit, and a rather abundant crop, at that. I'm more patient, kind, and gentle than when I was a parent. Of course, I can send our grandchildren home when they're fussy—a luxury I didn't have with our own kids. Still, I'm mellower now.

It's profoundly humbling yet deeply satisfying to be producing spiritual fruits. Thank you, Lord, for being patient with me through the years. My grandchildren thank you too.

GIVING GENEROUSLY,
GIVING WISELY

It is possible to give away and become richer! It is also possible to hold on too tightly and lose everything.
—*Proverbs 11:24 TLB*

Assist me, O God, in giving generously of these things—time and energy, affirmation and affection, laughter and joy. May I never be miserly with any of the gifts you've given me. Especially let me be generous to my grandchildren. I do not wish to cater to their every whim. I want to bless them in ways that lead to their growth—that will bring forth respect, responsibility, and reverence. I already have too many of this world's goods. Open my heart and let me give, that I may become an ever-richer person and grandparent.

GRANDPARENTS
ARE IMPORTANT

*Grandchildren are the crown of the aged, /
and the glory of children is their parents.*
                                    —*Proverbs 17:6*

Successfully raising children is a group effort. We grandparents can be very important components in the process. We're not just extra-added attractions, frosting on the cake. You, O God, have given us a significant role to play. We're living longer than ever. Opportunities are available for us as never before; we should be pleasantly assertive and make the most of them.

Our grandchildren need us. Who else will teach them how to look through a kaleidoscope, play marbles, create sidewalk chalk art, use a yo-yo, build snowpeople, or wash dishes in the sink? And we need *their* energy and enthusiasm. We're a perfect match!

GRANDPARENTS' PRAYER

"Whoever welcomes one such child in my name welcomes me."
—*Matthew 18:5*

O God of all nations and peoples, prepare a welcome for our grandchildren when they venture forth into the world. Neither we nor their parents can go with them everywhere. We don't expect others to think they're beautiful, intelligent, and perfect, even though we're convinced they are. We hope and pray, however, that everyone they meet will accept them for who they are, will value their gifts and be kind and gentle to them. O gracious God, we do not ask you to give them special favors, but to protect them, give them confidence, and hold them in your hands. Let them know how very much they are loved!

GRANDPARENTING FROM AN ETERNAL VIEWPOINT

～

It is a wonderful thing to be alive! If a person lives to be very old, let him rejoice in every day of life, but let him also remember that eternity is far longer.
—*Ecclesiastes 11:7-8a TLB*

Being grandparents is a great responsibility and a pure delight. In this life, we and our grandchildren experience many small but painful separations—we or they go on vacation, they head off to college, one or the other of us moves to a different community. But deep down, "It is a wonderful thing to be alive!"

It's a high honor to be a grandparent. Yet sooner or later we shall be separated by death. "Grandpa" and "Grandma" will probably go first. It will hurt those left behind. So remind them frequently, O everlasting God, that though life can be wonderful, eternity is far longer and more glorious.